FAYRUZ

Where All That Is Lost

Can Be Found

By

Kobi Abramovich

WITCH

To The Grey Donkey, With Love And Longing.

Though they do not read books, it would be fitting to dedicate this book to all the grey donkeys—wherever they may be.

First, because they are creatures of unparalleled wisdom and humility.

Second, because their lot is a hard one, forced to eat straw and spend their days in toil.

With no one to understand them, grey donkeys have every reason to hide in the shadows, and for a long time, not one has been seen here. I grieve deeply for these wondrous donkeys. One donkey, dear to my heart above all—my grey donkey. This book is dedicated to him.

KOBI ABRAMOVITCH

1

Climbing mountains is a pursuit some take upon themselves, its sole purpose to conquer peaks. Thus, they spend their time wandering from mountain to mountain, seeking new summits to claim.

If you ask mountain climbers why they conquer peaks, they will surely say, "Because they are there." As if the conquest itself is their heart's desire. But the truth is, on their way to the peaks, they seek something they do not even know.

I, too, was a mountain climber—searching, with all my might, for something of that sort.

For many years, I wandered from place to place. I risked my life climbing peaks from which, I thought, one could see what cannot be seen from below. Until I reached the Galilee. From there, one can see far into the distance—what truly matters. The wondrous land, the hills, the sea, the sunset, and the next mountain.

This enchanted region was once the land of the wondrous donkeys... but now you will not find even a single grey donkey here. Wild donkeys, *alhamdulillah* (thanks God), are plentiful. They have been here since time immemorial. But a splendid grey donkey? You will not see one. The poor creatures are ashamed, retreating into the shadows.

2

In the beginning, there were no donkeys at all in the Galilee. Not until he arrived… Sultan al-Karim.

When Sultan al-Karim ("the Great Ruler") heard of the Galilee, a wondrous land with unique, industrious people who know how to love and are content with little, yet for some reason lack joy, he left all his affairs and came at once.

"Here is a rare opportunity to rid myself of goods no one wants," al-Karim thought to himself. What else was he to do with a herd of donkeys? Even a single donkey was hard to find use for. He had good intentions, this Sultan al-Rahman ("the Merciful Ruler"), but somehow, everything went awry…

And so he came, from the Lebanon Valley, striding beside a snow-white donkey, followed by a vast herd of white donkeys, prancing joyfully behind him. He passed through villages, promising the shepherds that nothing would bring them happiness, health, or even luck like these white donkeys of his.

Some were suspicious. The shepherds were no naive fools or *ahbal* ("witless"). Some claimed that al-Karim made up the story just to sell them his donkeys as quickly as possible. "What else is he to do with them?" they grumbled. "He bought a herd of wounded, neglected donkeys at a high price, restored them, and now he'll sell them to us cheaply and slip back to wherever he came from."

The beauty of the donkeys and the promise of happiness nearly overcame the shepherds' wariness. In the end, it was the low price of the donkeys that tipped the scales. The shepherds couldn't resist the temptation. After haggling, every shepherd bought a donkey. Each shepherd had one donkey, all of them identical and unremarkable.

Once the deal was done, the shepherds asked the cunning merchant to explain, with all due respect, how to care for this strange creature.

"Very simple," replied al-Kabir ("the Mighty"). "The more you love them, the greater the happiness they will bring you." And just before he turned to leave, he remembered something: "Feed them only straw and chaff," he said, "and give them a bucket of water."

3

After selling all his donkeys, al-Kabir returned, accompanied by his radiant she-donkey, striding toward the high mountain. The shepherds went back to their homes, each dragging a white, gleaming donkey behind them.

At first, they left the donkeys to themselves and waited patiently for some happiness. But what is bought cheaply holds little value in the eyes of the shepherds, and what happiness could they find in something worthless?

And the donkeys? They longed for their kin and the vibrant life of the herd. Their yearning tormented them, and they shook with great fury until they fled their new masters' homes, seeking one another. Great was their joy each time a donkey found its fellow. The shepherds, unaware of how loyal donkeys are, mourned those that had left.

"Who will bring us happiness now?" the shepherds asked their old *mukhtar* (village leader).

"*Ana mush -'aref*" (I don't know, I don't understand), he replied, dismissing their sorrow.

When the donkeys returned, the shepherds tied them with ropes to stakes, fences, or tree trunks—anything to keep them from leaving again. Now the donkeys, too, were sorrowful. For a donkey is a creature of freedom.

Time did its work, and the donkeys… did nothing. They brought no happiness to the shepherds.

"If not happiness," the shepherds thought, "at least let them be useful."

But what use could there be in a donkey?

"Perhaps we could ride them?" someone suggested. "Riding, if it takes the rider to their destination, has some use, and perhaps some happiness," said the shepherds, who could not distinguish between the two. But the donkeys were not meant for riding. There's no way to spur a lazy donkey toward an unclear destination, let alone make it gallop. At best, it might plod to the feeding trough or trudge to nowhere.

Later, the shepherds hitched the white donkeys to heavy millstones or iron plows. They loaded them with heavy burdens and tasked them with all manner of hard labor. The donkeys performed the work efficiently, to the best of their ability, out of love for the shepherds. For a donkey loves to love, and all it asks is for its shepherd to be happy.

The work in the Galilee was now done with great efficiency. For a time, the industrious shepherds were content, but happy they were not. The donkeys suffered, too. Being adaptable creatures, they adjusted to their grey lives, and slowly, their radiant coats turned ashen.

In their distress, they longed for Sultan al-Kabir, who, though he fed them straw and chaff (nonsense), knew how to love them as they were and cared for them so well that they became treasures. The donkeys daydreamed of distant, lofty mountains where they could live simple, beautiful herd lives as before, with Sultan al-Rahman as their shepherd.

Meanwhile, the shepherds doomed themselves to a life of hard work and sorrow over an unfulfilled promise of happiness. They neglected and abandoned the donkeys out of ignorance and unfortunate misunderstanding.

"Who has ever seen a donkey here?" say the shepherds of the Galilee, denying the legend of happiness.

"It's all lies! All *kalaam fahadi* (nonsense)!" they say in the local tongue.

"Tales brought by nomads from the far north. Baseless stories of some radiant, wondrous creature carrying the secret of happiness. Fairy tales!"

So the shepherds claim to this day, and no one knows what is truth and what is fiction.

4

Once, as I rested from my climb upon a sharp rock ledge, a girl sat beside me. A sorrowful-looking girl, clad in a shepherd's grey galabiya. Her face was veiled by a simple scarf, embroidered with crimson thread. Only her turquoise eyes, peeking through the fabric, glowed with a precious light.

"Have you seen my she-donkey?" she asked, hiding something behind her back. Then she steadied her breathing, calming a little from the effort of the climb.
I stayed silent. I had been climbing this cliff for days and hadn't seen a living soul.
"No..." I replied.
"Pity," she sighed. "If I don't find her soon, she'll vanish forever... And where's your donkey?"
"I don't have a donkey."
"Of course you do! And he's one of a kind, unique, unmatched among other donkeys," she said. She opened her turquoise eyes wide and looked straight into mine.
I lowered my gaze and pondered.

"I don't have a donkey," I whispered.

"Everyone has a grey donkey. And if they don't care for it, nurture it, it hides in the shadows."

"So what?" I asked.

"Oh... then it turns wild. The wild ones are ravenous, not as wise as their grey kin, and that's what drives them to climb mountains," said the shepherdess, lowering her gaze. The frayed end of a rope now peeked from her hidden hand.

"Is that what happened to your donkey?" I asked.

"She's a she-donkey," she corrected me. "And she roams the mountain peaks. A wild one, she is. She does only what she wants... and I... I search for her there."

Silence fell between us.

"I see... you carry worry in your heart," she said, pointing to the safety rope tied around my waist.

"I'm not worried."

"Then what's at the end of that rope?" she asked.

"The mountain," I replied, smiling. "I tied myself to the mountain."

"And how can mountains ease worries?" she asked, touching the small crease between my brows, the mark of every worrier.

"I'm a professional, skilled mountain climber," I explained. "I have no reason to worry. I take only calculated risks."

"Calculated risks?" she said with a sad smile.

"Calculations... they're truly dangerous! I'm sorry you must calculate risks and tie your worries with a rope and climb mountains... How great is the sorrow of mountain climbers..." she said, retreating into herself.

"When our donkey is wild, it might tempt us to climb mountains," she warned, raising a finger.

I was quiet for a moment, then explained that if you don't embark on climbing journeys, you'll never reach the peak.

"The peaks? They're treacherous!" she insisted. "Sometimes they don't keep their promises. But it's alright—if that's what your wild one wants, you must care for it."

"How do you care for a donkey?"

"You don't need to care for it. You need to cherish it and love it as it is."

She pulled a small piece of Rahat Lokum from her pocket, broke it in two, and offered me one half.

"That's all a shepherd's duty is…" she said, eating the other half herself.

5

We huddled on the edge of the narrow rock ledge, above the abyss, and ate the Lokum. Nothing dispels strangeness like a cube of Rahat Lokum.

I didn't ask the name of the girl beside me, and she didn't bother to introduce herself. The shepherds of the Galilee don't care much for names. The people themselves matter more. So she sat beside me, nameless, catching her breath from the climb that brought her here. And as we sat on the edge of the abyss, our closeness grew.

When the Lokum was gone, we talked more and more. About donkeys and desires. About fears and the dangers of mountain peaks. Only when it grew late and evening fell, just before darkness covered everything and the strangeness was forgotten, did the grey girl introduce herself to me:

"Well," she concluded, "you're a shepherd who, weighed down by worries, ties himself to rocks and cannot see his splendid grey donkey... And I am Fayruz."

"Pleased to meet you," I replied, smiling. "But I'm not a shepherd. I have no herd, never did. I'm a mountain climber."

"We're all shepherds. Even those who flee to seek treasures on mountain peaks. Not every shepherd has a herd," she explained. "I have only one radiant she-donkey, and I am her shepherd," she said with a sad smile.

"And what makes you a shepherd?" I asked cautiously.

At first, she was silent, embarrassed. "I don't know," she replied. "I'm a shepherd because I have a radiant she-donkey! And after she left, she left longing and worry in my heart. I'm her shepherd. Sometimes she's unbearable, and I don't understand her at all. But now that she's gone, I must find her before the storm wind reaches here. A shepherd is anyone with worry in their heart."

I didn't know what storm she meant. What had she lost that made her fear ropes and imagine a grey donkey? But my heart went out to the humble shepherdess whose whole world was one she-donkey, now lost. Where had her she-donkey gone? What had become of her? I didn't dare ask. And what of my own worry? Could it be that the worry once in my heart had faded? Had I already forgotten who or what I worried for? One thing I knew for certain: once, before I set out for the mountains, there was worry in my heart, or at least a longing for something. And what had become of that longing—I did not know.

"Why did she leave?" I asked carefully.

Fayruz was silent. "I'll help you find her," I promised, without knowing how. And so I found myself bound by worry to this girl with turquoise eyes.

6

The next day, as we descended the mountain, a green and splendid valley unfolded before us. The Valley of Blessing and Fortune. A valley brimming with nature's bounty —fields of wheat and barley, sprawling olive groves, orchards bearing fruit year-round, flocks of sheep, and shepherds in vast pastures. On the valley's edge stood a small village. Fayruz's village.

The village looked abandoned and sorrowful. The sharp smell of lingering smoke hung here and there. Overturned carts and uprooted belongings were scattered everywhere. On the path leading to the village center, Fayruz found a pair of gold earrings. She picked them up and gazed at them with pain. It seemed she recognized them, and they stirred a stinging memory… "What happened here?" I asked.

"It's the cruel storm wind," she said, her voice trembling.

The harsh sights of the ravaged village stirred memories of my past life. A life I left behind when I set out on this journey. Memories of the home I abandoned in my urge to chase new peaks and conquer them. And my loved ones? What remained of them? What remained of all that was dear to me? Lost? And where was all that was lost? Worry and longing filled my heart. What had happened to me? Surely some storm wind had struck me, too.

"Come. Let's ask Afifa," Fayruz requested after a long search through the empty alleys. "She was the last to see her before she was lost."

Afifa spotted us from her kitchen window and came out to greet us, waving her hands joyfully.

"My dear," Afifa called to Fayruz, waiting with open arms.

"Have you seen my she-donkey?"

"Yes," Afifa stammered as she hugged Fayruz. "She passed through here, stopped in the garden for a moment, then moved on. She'll return," Afifa promised. "Donkeys never abandon their home. No matter how far they roam, they always tread back home." It had been a long time since Fayruz had visited, and Afifa missed her dearly. "That naughty one ran off again?" Afifa asked.

"A strange creature," Afifa said to herself, returning to her soap-making. "You never know what she really wants. Why did she run off, and why did she come here, to my herb garden? And what made her, just now, continue on her way? What does she seek?"

But the she-donkey sought nothing for herself. Donkeys don't seek happiness or freedom. They are content as they are, so long as we accept and love them as they are. God made them thus—pure, simple, and true.

After pouring a few more soap molds, Afifa paused her work. She set down the greasy ointment, wiped her hands on her small apron, and went to make us black, sweet tea and sesame-honey cookies. Fayruz sat by the kitchen window and waited. In the distance, thunder rumbled, and heavy black clouds moved toward the village from the Lebanon Valley, heralding the return of the storm wind. What would become of the shepherds? And the herds?

7

As the storm wind threatened to return, and as Fayruz searched with all her might for something she didn't even know, a treasure revealed itself to her. A true treasure! When they wish, things reveal themselves right where we stand. One must be wise to notice them and claim them before they vanish forever.

It lay on the table in Afifa's small kitchen, as if waiting just for her. A small notebook, filled with drawings, formulas, and writings in faded ink, yet still legible with words of magic. All written with fine taste on yellowed, crumbling paper. Among its wondrous pages were dried flowers. There was even a map, drawn in red ink.

"What could be a greater treasure than this? If I could read what's written here, I might decipher these formulas and… that's it!" Fayruz said to herself, hiding her treasure in a fold of her galabiya as one conceals a dubious deed. Though she couldn't read or write, she knew deep within that a great treasure had fallen into her hands, and if she could find a way to read it, it might guide her to the place where all that was lost could be found. Thus, her adventure had begun, and who knew where it would lead her. And so, though she knew it wasn't hers, Fayruz took the notebook and its map for herself.

Afifa prepared provisions for our journey—a few remaining cubes of Rahat Lokum and an assortment of colorful, cheerful soaps. We thanked Afifa, bid her farewell, and continued on.

8

After Fayruz stole the small notebook, Afifa was at a loss. In that notebook, her kind grandmother had written, in her tiny handwriting, dozens of recipes for fragrant soaps and perfumes, and even a list of all the wild plants of the Galilee, with dried flower samples to aid identification. The notebook was written when important things were still recorded. Afifa knew it was a true treasure and guarded it as such.

The kitchen, filled with good scents and tools, came to a standstill. Afifa had devoted her life to turning her grandmother's small secrets into magic. Otherwise, she couldn't have turned fine olive oil and a few herbs into soap.

Since the notebook disappeared, her soap-making enterprise halted. She hadn't made Rahat Lokum in a long time either. The mastic trees, whose sticky resin made excellent sweets, had long vanished. Except for one lone tree standing on some distant peak in the north. So high was that peak, no one could conquer it without a donkey. The map showing the way to that mastic tree was lost with the recipe book, and without Rahat Lokum, there was nothing to bribe the grey donkeys with.

Afifa knew the demand for soaps depended not on their quality or scent but on their shape. Had her soap-making not stopped, she would have carefully crafted soaps in unique shapes—shells, leaves of the oriental plane tree, and other whimsical forms—never cubes! Lest someone mistake them for food.

9

We walked together toward the village center and sat by the drinking pool. Fayruz read from the notebook as if it were hers, while I filled our waterskins with cool water.

It was already autumn. The ground was covered with fallen leaves, perfect as bookmarks, and though she took care not to damage books, Fayruz folded a tiny corner of a page to mark her place and closed the notebook. Then, she tore out a page and drew something on it with a pencil.

In the village square stood an ancient, stooped mulberry tree. Somehow, this wise tree had survived the storm wind once again. At its foot sat the village *mukhtar* ("the chosen one") as always. "From here," he thought, "you see everything, know everything, understand everything. What makes me the mukhtar if not sitting here in the center of the square?"

Beside him gathered a few shepherds, each with a neglected grey donkey by their side.

"How are you?" Fayruz asked the mukhtar.

"Mmm..." he replied, half-asleep, without bothering to look at her. "*Alhamdulillah* (all is well, praise God). I just wonder... where have all our splendid donkeys gone?" he said.

"They're here. With you. Why do you ignore them?" Fayruz asked.

"Those aren't ours," the mukhtar replied. "Those are just plain, neglected grey donkeys. Ours were beautiful and radiant."

"Then what about all these?" Fayruz asked, pointing to the group of donkeys standing there.

"We have no need for them. They're the most idiotic creatures, good for nothing but chewing straw."

"And even the little they do is always tied to arguments and strife," added another shepherd. Such are the shepherds of the Galilee; that's all they could see in their lost donkeys.

"Yes! Yes!" a few shepherds agreed among themselves.

"Who needs donkeys like that?" said another, holding the frayed end of a short rope, its other end chewed. "In the end, the splendid ones always disappear."

After these words, silence fell over the village square. Fayruz hung her drawing on the trunk of the old mulberry tree.

"Did you lose a bird?" the mukhtar asked.

"It's my she-donkey," Fayruz replied. "That's how she looked through Afifa's kitchen window the day she ran off!"

"It still looks like a seagull to me," the mukhtar grumbled.

"That's because you only see what you want. Anyone with a donkey would recognize it at once."

"Since when do donkeys have wings?" the mukhtar growled. "That's all we need now—for them to start flying above us!" he said, covering his head with his hands, as one does in such situations...

"Where did she fly off to, that she-donkey of yours?" the mukhtar asked, smiling to himself. It's all fiction, he thought, there are no donkeys, and they certainly can't fly. If he smiled at her, perhaps he could ease her worry.

"I don't know," Fayruz replied, her heart heavy. "And she herself surely doesn't know where she is. I think she's waiting for me where all that is lost can be found," she tried to explain.

"Where do you get all this nonsense?" the mukhtar snapped.

"It's written in my notebook," she replied, as if it were obvious.

"Well, go argue with books," the mukhtar said, swatting an imaginary fly from his face.

"Your donkey is there, too…" Fayruz argued.

"I don't have a donkey. The village folk are enough for me. The last thing I need is a donkey of my own."

"Are you sure that's exactly how she looked?" the mukhtar asked.

"That's how Afifa saw her."

"Afifa! Afifa! What would we do without that Afifa?" the mukhtar exclaimed, clapping his hands.

"Then that's your she-donkey, as Afifa saw her, carried on the wings of your imagination," the mukhtar concluded as precisely as he could.

"More or less," Fayruz replied, smiling at the old mukhtar. Then she retreated into herself, mourning the she-donkey she had lost.

"Well, fine…" the mukhtar said, noting her silence. "The things we've lost are the dearest to us. Now that we've settled the matter of the ears, perhaps we should go look for her," he said, but did nothing. He had a few more questions.

Such are the shepherds of the Galilee—overwhelmed by worry, they ask and ask, seeking to see and know more and more instead of understanding the little they do see. So it is with their mukhtar.

"Come. Let's keep looking for her," I suggested to Fayruz, and we left the village square behind.

10

"They're good-hearted people," Fayruz said, pulling me aside. "They're hardworking, devoted, and loving." She tossed a yellow sorrel flower into the drinking pool in the village square and chewed its sour stem with relish. "They're good people, but the whole matter of the donkeys causes them great sorrow, and they're slowly sinking into self-pity." The small flower swirled and landed on the water's surface. Then it was carried away by the current, disappearing as we walked away.

"I don't understand," I said to Fayruz. "Why don't they see their donkeys?"

Fayruz opened her notebook and flipped through it, as if searching for the page with the right answer. "Here," she said, pointing to a passage written in faint, illegible handwriting. "Longing and sorrow blind the shepherds' eyes," she read, quickly snapping the notebook shut. "Understand?" she asked, straining to explain. "If they see it, they don't recognize it. They think it's someone else's donkey that lost its way and ended up here. They don't know it's their donkey. They deny it, and then they're filled with sadness and longing for the good donkey they once had. That's how they make themselves sorrowful. Running about all their days, from here to there, holding a rope tied to a neglected, miserable donkey, searching. Busy looking for something they don't even remember the look of, with no idea how they'll ever find it. What happiness can a shepherd who denies their donkey expect when that 'jewel' stands right beside them?" she asked, a half-smile on her lips.

"And the donkeys? What about them?" I asked.

"Donkeys!" she replied. "They never change. They tie themselves to the rope at the end of which is their neglected, miserable shepherd and wait with donkey-like patience until the truth comes to light. Meanwhile, no one mourns for them," she said, sorrow gleaming in her turquoise eyes.

The sun had set, the low clouds had scattered, and the silhouette of a great mountain's peak appeared before us in all its glory.

"There's the Rose of the Winds Mountain!" I exclaimed, pointing to its peak. How beautiful is a peak yet unconquered.

"Maybe my she-donkey is wandering there…" Fayruz suggested.

"Maybe," I said, smiling to kindle hope in her. For myself, I thought we might find nothing there.

A new peak always stirred excitement in me, seeming like an invitation to climb. I had scaled peaks loftier than this one without knowing why. But this time, I knew what I was searching for—Fayruz's she-donkey. And that hope thrilled me and called me to ascend.

"Tomorrow, at dawn, we'll go there together," I suggested, and she nodded in agreement.

11

Dawn broke, and the first rays of sunlight roused us from our sleep. We greeted each other and began preparing for a day of walking together.

The valleys and winding paths led us to a magnificent mountain. Fayruz shared that the shepherds call it "Rose of the Winds" because, on the maps of the Galilee, a wind rose is marked precisely where the mountain is drawn. "The shepherds love symbols and signs. With them, they know where they've been and where they're going, and they can see in them what they wish."

"And what does the Rose of the Winds symbolize?" I asked.

"The Rose of the Winds?... Just a moment," said Fayruz, searching for the entry in her notebook. "Well," she read solemnly when she found what she sought, "it is the name of a splendid mountain—those who tread its paths will notice that as the direction of their walk changes, so too does their state of mind."

It was a colossal mountain, with all four winds encircling it from every side. We climbed its spiraling path in silence, circling the mountain countless times as the shifting winds caressed us.

We met the eastern *Sharqiyah*, hot and dry, cracking our lips and filling our mouths and eyes with dust. After hours of walking along the mountain's western slope, the eastern wind ceased.

As we moved to the southern slope, the northern winds arrived. Cold and tempestuous, they struck us without mercy. Ill winds, carrying thoughts of dangers and miscalculations. Fayruz sank into a melancholic reverie about the storm wind threatening to harm her and all she held dear. I tried to comfort her, assuring her the wind would shift its course, and sorrow would turn to hope.

"It's not good to walk against the wind," she whispered to me.

The winds and scenery changed ceaselessly before our eyes, but the mountain itself remained unchanged.
Evening fell. A gentle western breeze brought it from the sea, accompanied by a noisy flock of seagulls and the scents of the sea and vast expanses yet to be explored. It was already late, and we still hadn't arrived.

We sheltered from the shifting winds behind a large rock slab, slipped into our sleeping bags, and fell asleep. The mountain winds never rest, ceaselessly changing. A southern wind caressed us in our sleep. Warm and gentle, it carried the howls of lost jackals, the screeches of predatory birds hunting their prey, and dreams. Sweet dreams of donkeys, desires, fears, dangers, and mountain peaks. Sweet dew dampened our sleeping bags, our sunburned faces, our backpacks, and our dreams. By morning, the dry eastern wind returned, drying everything with the rising sun and another day of exhausting walking. We marched determinedly, on and on, against the shifting winds, not knowing what they sought.

12

We climbed the mountain for many hours.
The changing scenery began to repeat itself.
"We're walking in circles," I complained.
"When we're lost and don't know how to choose,
our donkeys lead us round and round,"
Fayruz sang to me in a strange little tune.

"Going back to the same place is a waste of time," I grumbled. "We could have climbed the slope straight to the peak... I don't understand. Where are our donkeys taking us?"

"Sometimes I don't quite understand either," Fayruz admitted, explaining that no one knows what truly drives her wondrous, peculiar she-donkey. All she knew was that her she-donkey was sensitive beyond measure, both bold and fearful, and only one thing truly calmed her—love. Though love stirred her soul more than anything, she never had enough of it, and her search for love led her into all sorts of troubles...

Hearing this, I couldn't tell if Fayruz was speaking of herself or her she-donkey. In any case, I felt sorrow for both.

As our journey up the mountain continued, the circles tightened, and we grew accustomed to the shifting winds. Beyond themselves, they changed nothing. The true changes we wrought ourselves.

Before our legs nearly gave out, the spiraling path reached its end, and we found ourselves on the summit. There, on the barren, bald peak, we stood, weary and thirsty, filled with dreams, birds, and thoughts sown by the four winds. Thoughts of donkeys, desires, fears, dangers, and mountain peaks. But no she-donkey was there. Nor even plain grey donkeys. No view stretched out from there, only a misty cloud cloaking and hiding everything.

We longed for a gentle breeze to come from anywhere it pleased. How beautiful is the wind's power to clarify what is shrouded in mist.

When it didn't come, we stood on the peak, disappointed and weary, lost in ourselves and our sorrow, barely noticing the one standing beside us—a young shepherd boy dressed in a white robe, carrying a long herding staff. Sometimes sorrow and longing blind the shepherds' eyes.

13

The boy gazed down the mountain's slopes, preoccupied with his herd of donkeys climbing toward the peak.

"They're almost here," he said. We looked to the mountain's base, but nothing could be seen save heavy rain clouds carried by the sea wind.

"I must find her before it starts to drizzle," Fayruz said to the donkey herder. "My she-donkey doesn't like getting wet."

"You raise a very pampered she-donkey. My donkeys don't care about anything as long as they're together," the herder said, then called to his herd with encouraging shouts: "Haa... Haa... Pfft... Rrr!"

The herd of donkeys climbed slowly up the mountain, raising a thick cloud of trail dust into the air. A white aura enveloped the long caravan of donkeys, and the light clatter of their hooves grew closer. Tick, tack-tack, ting, tsk-tsk, and the sounds of crunching gravel on the winding path to the peak broke the evening's silence. Moments later, snorts, stomps, loud complaints, brays, and thuds followed... The commotion grew as the massive herd ascended toward the summit.

The first marchers already stood by the herder, and those behind them crowded in. Gradually, the herd transformed from a long caravan into a noisy, grey mass. Faint, small sounds of modest brass bells dangling from the donkeys' necks could now be heard. As delicate as the bells were, their chimes didn't soar or echo down the slopes but were absorbed into the donkeys' coats, becoming light metallic clinks. So humble were they.

Only when the entire herd completed the climb and emerged from the grey mist onto the mountain's peak did Fayruz notice them. They seemed to her like a vast flock of seagulls soaring above the cloud. A jubilant flock, bringing with it wherever it went a hefty dose of noise, zest for life, small intrigues, playful schemes, and countless little celebrations of camaraderie and shared fate. From all this, the grey donkeys crafted their donkey-like fellowship and joyful togetherness.

"Such a splendid, massive herd of donkeys I've never seen," said Fayruz.

14

"Are you lost?" the stranger asked us. He took a sip of water from a leather waterskin.

"No," Fayruz hurried to reply. "We climbed here searching for the she-donkey I lost."

"Somehow, I always find a few lost donkeys here," the boy said. "I gather them into my herd, and then we move on without lingering. We'll return here anyway."

"Have you seen my she-donkey?" Fayruz asked excitedly.

"What does she look like?"

"A donkey," Fayruz answered with a sad smile. "You can't mistake them. They're like no other."

"I have tons of donkeys here, all sizes and colors, every kind you can imagine. You can pick one. Whichever you want," the boy offered.

"But I'm looking for *my* she-donkey."

"What's special about her? They're all the same. Take another from my herd."

"She's mine," Fayruz replied. "And besides, she has eyes like mine

—turquoise. This big," she demonstrated with her clenched fists. "And they gleam." As she spoke of her she-donkey, Fayruz's eyes shone with the glow of those who know how to love their donkey. "Only I can love her as she needs. Without me, she's lost…"

The wind, which had already carried the dust cloud far into the abyss, now tugged the scarf from Fayruz's face. The donkey herder looked at her and, for a moment, forgot his shepherding duties…

"We'd better find her quickly," Fayruz said.

"Doesn't she know how to find her way home?" the herder asked. Fayruz thought to herself that perhaps she, too, wouldn't find her way home. Or maybe, in fact, she didn't want to return there without her beloved she-donkey. Then she flung the long end of her scarf over her shoulder, covering her flushed face…

"Maybe she's among them," the herder suggested. "Lost donkeys join this herd all the time."

"Have you seen her? Have you seen my she-donkey among them?"

"I don't know them all; there are too many, and they're so alike."

"But mine has a mark. Her eyes are turquoise," Fayruz reminded him.

"I don't know… they're always busy eating," he complained, "with their eyes closed."

"It depends on what you feed them," Fayruz replied, handing him a bag full of Rahat Lokum. The herder took one for himself and shared the rest with his donkeys. When the bag was empty, he regretted not feeding the entire herd with Rahat Lokum as he perhaps should have. He looked at Fayruz and saw her holding a rope, one end chewed, the other trailing an empty harness dragging on the ground.

"What's the point of a rope with no donkey at its end?" he asked her.

"It's a sign," Fayruz said. "A sign that I'm searching for my lost she-donkey. If, by chance, shepherds come across her, they'll remember the girl looking for her she-donkey… and maybe return her to me."

"Maybe there's no need for all that," the herder said. "They always come back home on their own."

"If I don't find her soon, she'll vanish. The purple thistles in the Galilee's pastures have grown so tall…" Fayruz said. "That's a bad sign."

"Why?" asked Musa.

"Because tall thistles mean no donkeys have grazed here for a long time."

15

When he finished tending to his massive herd and the grey, weary group quieted down, the herder sat beside Fayruz. There, in the shade of an ancient, wise olive tree, they huddled for a conversation. I watched the two young people engage in a Galilean shepherd's talk in a language I didn't understand. But I could see the love in the herder's heart and the great joy his grey donkeys brought him.

When they finished talking, they turned to care for the donkeys. They brushed their coats and wiped their eyes with a damp cloth. Then, Musa told us about his herd's story. It was a herd of unfortunate, wounded donkeys he had gathered on his journeys across the Galilee. Some limped, struggling to move from place to place. There were blind ones and those whose ears were lost in their owners' excessive efforts to teach them "proper behavior." Some bore burns or suffered terrible skin diseases. There were old ones and sick ones. Some had lost most of their teeth from age or hunger, unable to chew what the splendid pastures offered. There was even a donkey with a missing leg. I didn't dare ask what had happened to that leg. Some were too thin, others too fat. There were bald donkeys and shaggy ones smeared with paint. But a fine, well-groomed, festive donkey like the radiant she-donkey Fayruz had lost? Not one was there… Yet Fayruz saw none of this. In her eyes, they shared one thing—they were happy.

"They're so beautiful and unique," she said.

"Yes! They're one of a kind. But they're only beautiful if you love them."

"How can you not fall in love with them at once?"

"Those who nurture their donkey can't help but love it. But these…" Musa said, pointing to his herd, "are abandoned donkeys who've never known love. I collect them from backyards or mountain peaks and treat their wounds, burns, and scars. I relieve them of the heavy burden of unfulfilled dreams, disappointed loves, shame, and pain they carry on their backs in place of their shepherds. I brush their coats and make them happy. And when they're groomed, beautiful, and joyful—I return them home, to Sultan al-Karim. Because after all they've been through, they no longer know where they belong."

16

After these words, the young herder approached me and introduced himself. "Musa al-Ra'i (the Shepherd)," he said, warmly shaking my hand. "And you?"

"I'm a mountain climber."

"So am I," said Musa. "I climb mountains with my herd of donkeys."

I was thrilled to meet a fellow mountain climber. "What peaks have you conquered?" I asked.

"I'm a donkey herder, not concerned with conquests. I'm only occupied with loving my herd and wandering."

"What kind of job is herding donkeys?"

"It's not a job; it's a way of life. Though it's utterly simple, not everyone bothers to learn it. And those who choose it must do everything out of love for their donkey and surrender to its wandering life. Then, splendid adventures and a happy life await them."

"We both climb mountains," I suggested. "You herd your donkeys, and I search for…"

"What are you searching for?" he interrupted.

"The peak," I replied. But to myself, I thought I might not truly know what I'm seeking.

"In the eyes of donkeys, mountain peaks are no more special than any other place. They don't love things just because they're rare or unattainable. The high peaks are empty and desolate. They hold no hidden treasures. They're always lower than you thought, and your tiger will chase you there, too. Nothing pursues you more than what you seek to escape…

"But," Musa added, "if you climb out of love, if you're not afraid to look into the gaping abyss, then you can gaze at your peak and see how close you've come to it—and to the donkey within you."

Musa spoke more about the shepherd's duties, about donkeys, desires, fears, dangers, and mountain peaks. And I reflected on myself, the life I'd chosen, and what made me abandon what I once was—a shepherd with worry in his heart.

Fayruz listened to our talk and remembered her lost she-donkey. "I wasn't a worthy shepherd to her," she said sorrowfully.

"Deep down, everyone is an excellent shepherd," Musa told her. "Our donkeys love us just as we are and see us as worthy shepherds. That's how they are—beautiful, wise, and misunderstood."

We stayed with Musa's donkey herd on the mountain peak for a few more days, dedicating them to rest and caring for the donkeys.

When the skies cleared and no clouds remained, the herd began to gather. They seemed to be preparing for something. They clustered into a determined grey mass, braying and stomping impatiently. The donkeys had resolved it was time to descend the mountain. With no choice, we decided to go down, too, and continue searching for Fayruz's she-donkey and other abandoned donkeys in the Valley of Blessing and Fortune.

We hadn't yet gathered our packs when the excited herd lost patience and began marching toward the valley on their own.

"Just a moment," the herder pleaded. "I need to count you." Musa approached the last donkey in the herd and began counting.
"How many are there?" I asked, thinking he'd finished.
"Not enough…" he muttered. "I never manage to count them. They keep moving from place to place."

17

The three of us followed the herd down the mountain. Echoes of explosions rolled through the valley, shaking the ground. Sounds of a terrible war that refused to be forgotten. We walked, each lost in our own thoughts of what we had lost. Amid the war's clamor, the clatter of donkey hooves, and the cloud of dust they raised, Fayruz told us the story of her she-donkey.

She began with the foothills surrounding her village. There, in winter, stunning carpets of purple thistles bloomed. They were perhaps what her she-donkey loved to chew most of all. Her thick, strong tongue and tough coat spared her the pain of the thorns' pricks, and their taste was even lovelier to her than their appearance. She never saw them up close anyway, as she always closed her eyes before nearing the prickly flowers. Their vibrant purple didn't impress her much either. Donkeys only distinguish shades of brown and grey. Colors, however beautiful, don't confuse them.

"I don't know," Fayruz said, "what draws my she-donkey to mountain peaks. Melancholy sunsets or enchanting views don't interest donkeys at all. They don't value things for their beauty but for their quality. The sun, for instance—though shepherds find it more beautiful at sunset—donkeys prefer it at noon, when it's larger, closer, and so pleasantly warm. The farther it is, the less it interests them, no matter how beautiful. Donkeys!"

"But," she added, "I love my she-donkey and always let her choose where we'd go."

18

One morning, Fayruz recounted, as her she-donkey led them to a soft patch of grass, a tiger leapt from the bushes. It was their first time seeing a tiger up close. Some sights are once-in-a-lifetime. A tiger's sight might be one of them. A complex, majestic, terrifying, and unique creature. Fayruz knew how dangerous a tiger was and was terribly frightened. When the tiger leapt from the bushes, something in her contracted painfully. It wasn't just the immediate fear of the beast; it was a familiar, aching helplessness, returning suddenly like an old memory that refused to be forgotten. The tiger's form, its piercing green eyes, reminded her of other experiences—days when she couldn't escape, couldn't protect herself, and had no one by her side.

But her she-donkey knew none of this and felt no fear. She gazed at the tiger and saw a beautiful, noble creature standing in an odd pose. Perhaps trying to impress or charm? With a heart full of goodness, never having encountered evil, the she-donkey didn't know how to distinguish good from bad. And how terrible the beautiful can be!

The tiger's green eyes fixed on the she-donkey—what did it see? Even if hungry, it didn't see a meal. It saw a game. A splendid game invented by nature, with these rules: if the one before it flees, the tiger will chase and overpower it. That kind of game. The winner moves to the next stage, the loser leaves the game—forever!

To the tiger, nothing matters more than the need to play and amuse itself. Though it had tried many times to abandon the dreadful habit of hunting, it couldn't control itself in such moments. When a creature flees, the tiger thinks it wants to be chased and caught. So it immediately breaks into a swift run. Once the chase begins, there's only one way to end it—the tiger always catches its prey. When blood flows from the wounded creature, the scent of iron fills the air, reminding the tiger of the taste of flesh. Tigers love meat. In fact, they can't eat anything else...

But Fayruz's she-donkey didn't know this game's rules or anything about it. She stood her ground, head tilted, as if trying to understand something only she could see. "Come on!" Fayruz shouted, pulling the rope. But the she-donkey didn't budge.

The winds blew stronger, and the shadows around them deepened. Fayruz felt panic creeping into her heart. The she-donkey feared nothing and never bothered with running. If there's no running, there's no game. And if there's no game, what of the tiger? What of it? Why had it crept and slunk all night to this peak if not to devour whoever stood there and think itself successful in life?

The tiger was confused. It bared its teeth and growled to remind the she-donkey of its role in the game. She was utterly unimpressed by the tiger's display. She closed her eyes and turned her backside to the pompous tiger. It was now clear to the tiger that it wouldn't devour this donkey. It stood there a moment longer, insulted, then turned and slunk away.

One must respect the game's rules!

"You should have known I can't rely on you," Fayruz whispered angrily to her she-donkey. "You're useless." The radiant she-donkey, accustomed to being misunderstood and shunned, was unmoved by Fayruz's words. In any case, she likely had plans of her own. She lifted her head from the purple thistles, looked at Fayruz with a forgiving, loving gaze, and continued chewing. Fayruz looked into the she-donkey's turquoise eyes and remembered the storm wind… She grabbed the rope tied to the halter and pulled hard. "Yalla, Ruhi (Come on, go away)!" she shouted, yanking the rope. "Ruhi min hon (Get out of here)! Ruhi lil-baytak (Go to your home)!"

Suddenly, the ground shook—or so it seemed. The she-donkey raised her eyes, looked at Fayruz for a single moment, and then—like a dream disturbed—vanished. Fayruz returned home without her.

"She'll come back on her own," she thought to herself.

19

Many days passed, and the she-donkey didn't return. Fayruz went searching for her on paths and pastures but found no trace. She tried looking where she had vanished, but aside from a pile of fresh dung, she found nothing. Then she climbed the splendid mountain—Rose of the Winds—for hours. Her radiant she-donkey, though considered nearly blind and avoiding unnecessary effort, loved wandering the mountains alone. She'd choose a mountain, climb to its peak, stand there for hours, ears pulled back, gazing wisely into the distance. After a few hours, she'd retrace her steps.

Fayruz summoned her courage and climbed the mountains in her wake, treading the winding, steep paths alone. Even there, on the peaks, she found nothing. No she-donkey, not even dung.

Worry filled her heart. She so wanted to call her back, to promise never to scold her again, to bring her sweet carrots instead of the straw she chewed most of the day, which hurt her eyes until they blinded her. She wanted to shout, "Come back! I love you and miss you so much." But it was too late to say any of this.

"I should have told her I loved her before she vanished," Fayruz said to herself before descending the mountain. "And now I have no one to whisper to." She couldn't even call her, for she had no name. Still, Fayruz stood at the cliff's edge and shouted hoarsely, "She-donkey!"

"Doooonkeeeeey…" The echo rolled down the slope, fading until silence reclaimed the cliff and the valley below. Then Fayruz returned home, sad and disappointed.
"Don't worry, they always come back," her father assured her. "On their own."
"But she's nearly blind," Fayruz reminded him. "How will she find her way back?" Her father, though he heard, didn't answer. "She was useless anyway," he muttered aloud. "Allah yirhamha (May God have mercy on her)," he said, dismissing her and returning to his affairs.

Much time passed, and the beloved she-donkey didn't return. Sometimes, when filled with longing and sorrow, Fayruz returned to the places they'd spent together—the purple thistle fields, the peaks overlooking vast distances, the thorny raspberry bushes… No more donkey dung was seen in those places, and the purple thistles grew taller. Slowly, she despaired of ever finding her beloved she-donkey.

Time passed, the she-donkey was forgotten, and Fayruz became a shepherd haunted by longing and pain wherever she went. She couldn't overcome her longing through forgetting. The yearning for something already forgotten weighed on her heart, and her search for what she'd lost continued without knowing exactly what she sought, just like the other shepherds of the Galilee.

Thus, the young shepherdess wandered among the Galilean villages, trying to recall what she'd lost—until she stumbled by chance upon the remnants of the rope to which her she-donkey had been tied before she vanished.

20

For a mountain climber, there's little to seek in the Galilee. Most of its mountains aren't suited for climbing. They lack impressive peaks or spiraling paths, only humble, flat hills hiding nothing, certainly no treasure. But now, as I became a partner in the search for Fayruz's she-donkey and in gathering the neglected donkeys of the Galilee into Musa's herd, the wildness within me began to calm.

Those who don't herd flocks farm the Galilee's hills. The modest hills allow industrious farmers to build stone terraces and grow small barley fields or olive trees. On one such flat hill, Tallal Abu-Nimr had built an enclosure and raised a few donkeys. Musa told us Abu-Nimr's donkeys were in danger. We went there to try to save the donkeys trapped within.

"There are those in the Galilee who desperately want to ride a tiger or at least tame it," Musa told us. "But no one has truly managed to ride a tiger except Abdullah Qasem Muhamed (that was Abu-Nimr's name before he met the tiger). He rode a tiger down the wadi for 70 meters—the longest anyone ever rode a tiger. In fact, he rode it only half the time, as for the other half, they tumbled together down the slope, sometimes one on top, sometimes the other. It continued until Abdullah drew his dagger and stabbed the tiger. Then they lay bleeding side by side, waiting for help. With no one to aid them, they helped each other. The tiger cared for Abdullah because, without him, no one would see it, and it needs someone to flee from it to hunt. Abdullah cared for his tiger because he knew well that if something happened to it, he'd have nothing left to fear. Abu-Nimr took his wounded tiger to his small farm and nursed it back to health. Once it recovered, he set it free. For after growing accustomed to fear, it became a thrilling, addictive rush he couldn't resist. Without that thrill—who was he? The things we pursue - pursue us in turn.

"Since that event, he calls himself Abu-Nimr," Musa said, pointing to Abu-Nimr's enclosure.

When we arrived, Abu-Nimr was sitting on a woolen rug, sipping black coffee from a tiny cup, planning his next hunt. Hearing the commotion we caused; he ran from his hut and climbed the ancient olive tree at the enclosure's entrance. It was an empty yard, surrounded by barbed fences.

Seeing us, Abu-Nimr raised both hands and shouted, "Ya Allah!"—as the faithful in the Galilee call to God—"I asked for a tiger, and you sent me donkeys!" Then he laughed his rolling laugh and jumped from the tree to the ground. "Ahlan wa-sahlan (Welcome)!" he called to us. "Come in. My home is your home," he declared, opening the enclosure's gates.

The donkeys, realizing the gates were opened for them, rushed in joyfully. They had no idea what to do here or why they'd come, so they did what they knew best—chewed the soft grass. After the entire massive herd entered the enclosure, the shepherds asked Abu-Nimr to close and lock the gates. The donkeys didn't mind at all, for their disposition is always good, their spirit calm and serene. As long as they have grass or something to chew, it hardly matters where they are.

Abu-Nimr invited us into his home, seated us on a mat, and poured us cool water from a black clay jug. Then he served a royal feast with plenty of olives, pitas, and splendid goat cheeses. We drank black coffee together and talked with our generous host about donkeys and our herd's journeys across the Galilee. When the desserts were finished, Abu-Nimr excused himself and went to the yard "just for a moment" but didn't return even after an hour or two.

"Very strange," Fayruz whispered to us. "On our way here, we didn't meet a single donkey, and the enclosure is completely empty…"

"And it's quiet here… eerie and dangerous," Musa added. "And when Abu-Nimr poured our coffee, I noticed three fingers missing from his right hand."

Fayruz went to look for our host. She wandered the yard and, passing under the ancient olive tree, heard a rustle among the branches. She looked up but couldn't make out what she saw. "Musa!" she whispered. "Is that you?"

"Shhh… I'm lying in wait for my tiger," Tallal Abu-Nimr whispered from the branches. "When it comes, I'll jump onto its back and try to ride it again," he said, descending from the old olive tree.

"Why are you trembling?"

"I'm scared and excited."

"What are you scared of?"

"I'm scared of my boredom and excited for my meeting with my tiger."

"Do you have a tiger?"

"Everyone has a tiger! But if you choose to turn your back on it, you can't see it."

"I saw my tiger once," Fayruz said. "It happened only once, and it was frightening and dangerous. I wanted so badly to run, but my she-donkey refused to move. She stood and looked at it. In her eyes, it looked thin, hungry, and scared, with good turquoise eyes, like mine," she said, pointing to her own eyes. "My tiger lurks for me at every corner, but it's not dangerous at all. When I look at it, I'm not afraid of it," Abu-Nimr said. "In any case, I never run from it, because that's when it becomes dangerous," he said, crossing his arms behind his back, lost in thought. "They come in times of danger, especially when we think we're alone. It comes to protect me. But sometimes it comes for no reason at all… like that tiger of yours."

"How do you know it was my tiger?" Fayruz asked.

"It's simple," Abu-Nimr replied. "Everyone can only see their own fear."

I should have stayed and faced it, Fayruz thought. Maybe that's what my she-donkey did… The thought of her wise she-donkey, perhaps sacrificing herself to save her from death, shook Fayruz to her core.

21

The next day, it was Musa's turn to tend to the donkey herd, while Fayruz went with Abu-Nimr to pick black figs in the wadi. On the way to the wadi, Fayruz told Abu-Nimr about Musa and his vast herd. "I think I love them very much," she confessed, and Abu-Nimr listened attentively.

"They're useless creatures," Abu-Nimr scoffed after a long silence.
"But they know how to be joyful, they're good friends, and Musa is an excellent shepherd. They're happy with him, and because of them, he's so content… and they have so many wonderful dreams of journeys to distant mountains and…"
"You can't even ride them, and you certainly can't get anywhere with them," Abu-Nimr grumbled.
"You can go wherever you want with them and fulfill any dream, but only if you trust them."
"Trust donkeys?!" Abu-Nimr exclaimed. "I have no trust in my tiger. You can play with it, you can ride it, but you must be very careful. And dreams? Beware of dreams…" he said, waving his wounded hand toward her. "My dreams are more dangerous than

my tiger—they can't be seen."

"I see them clearly," Fayruz replied, "just as you see your tiger. It's my she-donkey I haven't seen in a long time."

"Shepherds are strange creatures," Abu-Nimr said. "They only see what they want and live dangerous lives of dreams, love, and wandering. And love is even more dangerous than a tiger because it only comes for a brief visit, and when it leaves, it leaves behind piles of dung."

"You mean piles of longing," Fayruz corrected him.

"I mean," Abu-Nimr said, "that wandering is a way of life where you choose to move constantly from here to there, searching for a place you know nothing about. Shepherds wander only because they hope the place they're going to is better than where they are."

"But…" Abu-Nimr added, "wandering is beautiful for those who dream awake."

"Who are the ones who dream awake?"

"Those who look straight at their dream."

"Then I'm a dreamer awake," Fayruz declared. "But I don't want to wander," she said. "I only hope to find my lost she-donkey and go back home."

Fayruz grasped Abu-Nimr's two remaining fingers as if they were rabbit ears.

"It still hurts," Abu-Nimr said, freeing his wounded hand from her grip. "Every dream has a price," he said, explaining that he lost his missing fingers in the jaws of his tiger.

"I'm sorry."

"No need. It's just the small price I paid to ride my tiger. Besides these two, I still have five more, not counting the ten on my feet. I could manage with just one," he laughed loudly, raising his finger to show Fayruz he still had all he needed.

22

"Do you think Musa dreams awake?" Fayruz asked Abu-Nimr.

"Yes," he answered simply.

"All shepherds dream and wander. They're always in a hurry to move from one pasture to another, as if there's a better field than the last. They have no time to settle in one place and discover its virtues. Flaws are obvious and immediately revealed," Abu-Nimr said, waving his rabbit-like hand again, "while virtues only show themselves with time," he said with his characteristic smile.

Hearing this, Fayruz grew very sad. If this man, whose heart no longer held love, was right, then parting from Musa and the donkey herd she loved so much was inevitable.

When they returned from the wadi, Fayruz approached Musa and asked if he, too, lived a life of wandering.

"Yes," Musa replied. "All shepherds wander."

"Don't you like it here?" Fayruz asked, her heart heavy with sorrow.

"I love it here, and how fortunate I am to have met you."

"Then why do you want to wander away from me?"

Musa fell silent.

"Because I care," Musa said, trying to ease her sadness. "That's what makes me a shepherd."

"What's wrong with the pastures here for your donkeys?" Fayruz pressed, hoping to change his mind.

"Nothing's wrong with them. They're excellent. I don't worry for myself or the donkeys. I care for us and love us with all my heart. I worry for the shepherds—those who lost these donkeys and seek a bit of happiness and comfort. We must find them and return what they've lost."

"It seems wandering has no end," Fayruz said.

"True," Musa replied, "and neither does caring."

Fayruz lowered her gaze and fell silent. *I was too busy with myself and my pampered she-donkey,* she thought.

"Do you think we can still wander together?" she asked.

Musa withdrew into himself, lost in daydreams. When he stirred, he said to Fayruz:

"I think... you need to find your she-donkey and wander after her. Every shepherd must follow their donkeys."

"But I love you and your donkey herd."

"Then," Musa said, "it seems we're in for days of mixed feelings."

"Mixed feelings?" Fayruz asked. "What's that?"

"It's when one shepherd's feelings blend with another's. You miss what you left in another shepherd's herd, yet you're happy for the wonderful things they left with you."

"Is that good?" she asked.

"It's what makes us who we are. That's how I carry longing and sweet memories from all the shepherds I've met on my wandering journey, and it makes me who I am."

"How beautiful is the wandering life," Fayruz exclaimed joyfully.

"I'll always remember," she promised Musa, "that maybe the feeling I carry was once yours, and maybe some of my feelings are now with you. How much happiness there is in mixed feelings."

23

Musa pulled a pocketknife from his pocket. He searched for a suitable reed among the rushes growing by the stream. He cut a reed and pierced it with a few holes. Then he covered some of the holes with his fingertips, closed his eyes, and blew into the flute, which began to play for him…

As Musa played, a tender and unique melody filled the entire valley, one Fayruz had never heard before. A clear sound carried on the wings of a great, silent wind. The donkeys stopped chewing, pushing, complaining, and clattering. They raised their heads from the grass, tilted their curious ears toward Musa, and listened intently to his flute's tune. Musa's flute produced magical, delicate sounds that, to the grey crowd, seemed like an ancient bray they might have heard in wonderful, distant places. Each donkey recalled what made them unique. Each remembered their previous herd and shepherd, from whom they came and to whom they'd surely return at journey's end. The melody grew, its notes rolling across the pasture, filling it, then spilling into the wadi and the mountains until everything was song. Slowly, the melody faded, the sounds merged into one delicate, precise, and quiet note until it fell silent entirely. A calm silence settled over the donkey herd, the pasture, and the shepherds. Loneliness was no more.

Fayruz asked Musa for the flute.
"It's hollow and empty," she said after examining it and handing it back to him.
"It's just a cut reed," Musa said. "All things, on their own, are nothing. You must fill them with a shepherd's song."
Fayruz took the flute again. She blew into it, filling it with air, but aside from the sound of blowing, no melody came.

"It's not enough to blow into it," Musa explained. "The flute's sounds are mere whimpers. Every shepherd has a unique tune in their heart, and they must blow it through their flute. Then everything is filled with the shepherd's song, and things become what they are."
Fayruz closed her eyes and listened to the melody in her heart. Then she blew into Musa's flute the ancient tune within her—a one-of-a-kind melody, even when it repeats, where everyone can hear what they wish. Fayruz listened to her tune and found her own beauty in it. Then she handed the pierced reed back to Musa and said, "Its name suits it—flute ('beautiful' in the local tongue). And how beautiful is the sight I saw through it."

Shawals (Lucky), who stood nearby chewing, had no interest in the shepherds' breath blowing through cut reeds or the music they made together. So he snatched the flute from Musa's hands, chewed it thoroughly, and swallowed it. A moment later, a joyful bray came from his mouth, as if the flute's melody was playing within the mischievous donkey. Then he moved on to find something else worth chewing.

"What a rascal," Fayruz said, laughing heartily.
"If you don't watch them, they sometimes do foolish things," Musa

said, embarrassed by his donkey's antics.

24

The next day, Musa and Fayruz bathed the entire herd. Before we set out to continue our wandering journey, we went to bid farewell to Abu-Nimr and thank him.

"I once had a donkey like that," Abu-Nimr said, pointing dismissively at one of the grey donkeys. To him, they were all the same—slow, boring creatures. "Truth be told, I had three like that. I bought them at an outrageous price, and they stood in the enclosure, braying endlessly. But a few nights later, my tiger came to visit, and the donkeys suddenly fell silent and disappeared. I haven't seen them since."

When Abu-Nimr mentioned his tiger, a big smile spread across his face, and for a brief moment, he was happy again.

"I always wanted a tiger," Abu-Nimr said. "A big, dangerous one. But I didn't know where to find such a beast. Once, a cunning trader passed through here with a large herd, much like yours. He offered to sell me some of his donkeys.

'I don't want any donkeys,' I told him.

'You don't want them, but you definitely need one. Oh, you do!' he said, and I heard him mutter to himself, 'They don't even know what they need.'

'Tell me... do you want a tiger?' the trader asked me.

'Yes!' I answered immediately.

'Well then,' he growled after a moment, 'you need a donkey! There's no prey tigers love more than innocent donkeys. Buy a donkey, and you won't need to bother about the tiger—just wait patiently. Where there's a donkey, a tiger will come.'

'How much does such a donkey cost?' I asked the trader, though I wasn't interested at all.

'I set a price for each buyer,' he replied. 'I need to get to know you before I can decide what price suits you.' For a long time, he questioned and probed me, drank tea, ate dried sesame cookies, and toured the enclosure I'd built for my tigers.

'It looks like a promising business... you could fill it with dozens of tigers,' he said, thinking I'd fall into his trap.

'Alright, so how much does such a donkey cost?' I asked as my patience wore thin.

'Now that you really want a donkey...' he began, twirling his mustache to set my price. 'How much are you willing to pay?' he asked finally. 'It's very important to me that you're satisfied.'

I offered him 14 dinars—double what everyone here paid for such donkeys. I was ready to pay twice that to meet a tiger.

'You'd better raise your offer,' he suggested, pulling his mustache upward. 'At such a low price,' he explained, pulling it back down, 'you won't be satisfied with the deal.'"

Fayruz knew nothing about trading, and the calculations of what was, what is, and what remained confused her. She couldn't figure out if Abu-Nimr's deal was worthwhile. But she felt sorry for the pain that deal had left in the hands of their generous host.

Musa and Fayruz lowered their gazes and fell silent. Worry crept into Fayruz's heart again, fearing her she-donkey might have fallen prey to a tiger.

"I think tigers don't even like donkey meat," Abu-Nimr tried to reassure them, but everyone knew he was lying.

"So, how much does a donkey like that cost?" Abu-Nimr asked them.

"They're not for sale," Fayruz replied. "Each one has someone waiting somewhere who truly loves them."

"Pity," Abu-Nimr said. "Pity. Farewell, strange bunch," he growled, waving his wounded hand at us.

"And if you meet a tiger, don't turn your back on it. If you do, it grows and becomes dangerous. But the closer you look at it, the smaller it gets," he added at the last moment. "But my tiger never shrinks—it's big, strong, and nothing is faster," he muttered to himself.

"Did you mean the tiger, or did you mean fear?" I asked him.

"It's the same thing," Abu-Nimr said, turned his back to us, and walked away.

"I don't like Abu-Nimr's tiger. It's wild…" Musa said when we were far from Abu-Nimr's hill.

"The role of our tigers is to protect us from danger," Fayruz read from her notebook.

"You're reading it upside down," Musa said, turning the notebook for her.

"It doesn't bother me," Fayruz said, continuing to read aloud: "If you look at them wisely, they shrink until they become worries. And worries are wise and seek only good. From worry, even the smallest, grow the greatest loves and mixed feelings," she said, hiding her face in her grey scarf.

"But if you don't watch the tiger, it becomes dangerous," she whispered. "And with the righteous storm wind, they turn into hunters. That's what makes their tigers devour, harm, and destroy everything."

25

As we progressed, our donkey herd grew. All sorts of donkeys joined us—some that had been attacked by tigers and survived, victims of others' fears, in all sizes and colors. Some had fled homes that disappointed them, joining our grey donkey herd. Others had endured unimaginable abuse, their owners bringing them to us themselves. To these sad shepherds, Fayruz gave pure olive oil soap, made by the kind-hearted Afifa, to comfort their aching hearts.

"How much wisdom and compassion Afifa brewed into her soaps," I thought to myself. "And who protects her? How does she cope with the storm wind?" And more worried, longing thoughts.

Each day, Fayruz counted the donkeys in the herd. She wiped their eyes, caressed each one's forehead, and whispered a magical, wondrous spell to them. The herd was so vast that Fayruz spent most of her day with the donkeys.

"We must care for them well, these innocent donkeys," Fayruz said, "both from the shepherds' negligence and the straw that blinds their eyes."

"And from the tigers," Musa added, "or we'll be left with only fears."

"While we care for our donkeys, our tigers protect us. If we don't let them devour, the fears give up and go seek easier prey elsewhere," Fayruz read from Afifa's secret notebook.

"On second thought, these donkeys aren't even ours," Musa corrected. "But as long as they wish, I'll be their shepherd. I don't need to own a donkey to love it. It's enough that I care for it. And if I care, I worry for it, and when I worry, I become its shepherd, and when I'm its shepherd, I learn to love it, and when I love it, I give it my Rahat Lokum, and then we're both happy." At this torrent of words, we all laughed.

Fayruz moved among the grey donkeys, hugging and petting each one. She wiped their wounded eyes from overeating, felt their necks, and adjusted the small bell tied to each one. Who knows? Perhaps the tiny bell could summon help for a silent donkey in a moment of danger.

"It's a good opportunity to count them," Fayruz suggested as we carefully crossed a small stream. She counted them, one by one. "176," she called to Musa after the last donkey crossed the stream. "Now it's your turn to watch them," she requested, descending back to the wadi to wash in its cool waters. "I knew from the first moment you were a wonderful shepherd," Musa said, knowing his friend couldn't hear him. "176... that's exactly enough," he said. "It's time," he called to Fayruz, who already felt the approaching farewell.

26

"There's one more donkey we need to pick up from the oil press," Musa said, remembering the donkey toiling there in hard labor.

"I always forget to collect him and remember just before it's too late," Musa apologized. "Poor thing." But by the time the entire group reached the oil press, it was already too late. No sound of grinding stones came from the press. Silence.

The exhausted miller sat by the millstones in a vast pool of olive oil. Around him were scattered dozens of broken clay jars. On one side was a huge pile of olives; on the other, his weary donkey lay. "I don't need a new donkey anymore," he mumbled with his last strength. "I'll make do with this one," he said, petting his donkey sprawled on the ground.
"What's all this? What happened here?" Musa asked the miller.
"Olive oil," the miller replied. "I thought I'd get rich," he wailed, splashing oil on the wall. "But you can't eat it, you can't drink it, you can't bathe in it, and there's nothing to do with it. I'm old now,

and it seems I've spent my life grinding between millstones like olives, and this is all I got—pure olive oil."

Musa dipped a finger in the oil pool and tasted it.

"It's excellent oil!" he said. "If consumed in the right measure."

Fayruz approached the miller, wiped his eyes with the hem of her galabiya, then caressed his forehead and offered him a small cube of Rahat Lokum. "I spent my life circling after these foolish beasts and got nowhere," the miller complained after chewing his Lokum.

"It seems to me you've finally arrived," Fayruz told him, removing the yoke from the weary donkey's back and placing a red headscarf on its head. "You have all you need," she said, handing him a rope with his tired donkey at its end. "Care for him," she suggested to the miller, "and he'll care for you."

"They don't know what they really need," Musa said as we left the oil press. "They're interested in what others have and grow jealous. Their grey donkeys are humble and want only good for them, but they don't listen or understand them. What do they need besides the donkey they already have?"

But I thought to myself that the old miller already knew this, and I hoped with all my heart that this time he'd dedicate his time to nurturing and loving his loyal donkey.

27

"Tomorrow, I'll sell the grey donkeys to the Sultan and part with the herd," Musa said. He spread an old camel-wool rug on the ground and prepared for the night's sleep.

"Why are you parting with them?" Fayruz asked.

"They no longer need me. They've known my love, heard all my flute's melodies, and are sated with Rahat Lokum, soft grass, purple thistles, straw, and chaff. There's not a single pasture in the Galilee we haven't grazed together. Their time has come to guide other shepherds."

"And what about you?" I asked.

"I'll wander to another land. There, I'll gather a herd of neglected donkeys who've never known love and be their shepherd."

"Maybe we should wash them first to increase their value," Fayruz suggested.

"He loves them as they are," Musa said. "When they're neglected, their value drops, so he can sell them to shepherds at very low prices. Besides, he truly loves them as they are. He says they don't carry value for us—they carry our dreams of what's possible."

"Tell us more about the Sultan," I requested.

"Gladly," Musa replied. He sat on his bedding and recounted:

"Sultan al-Karim always has a vast stock of grey donkeys. He buys them from shepherds who've completed their wandering journeys, when they're tired and worn from the trek. Then their price is lowest. In any case, Sultan al-Karim redeems the poor donkeys at any price, ready to pay whatever is asked. Then he takes them to his farm on a high, strange mountain. He rehabilitates them, loves them, and nurtures them until they become, in his eyes, radiant and precious. When he thinks their value has risen, he sells them cheaply to shepherds. He repeats this over and over, hoping one day to find shepherds who'll appreciate them—shepherds who won't seek utility in them and will finally understand that donkeys carry their happiness if only they're nurtured and loved.

That's how the Sultan buys flawed goods at a high price and sells fine goods cheaply. But to him, it's a worthy long-term investment. 'Donkeys,' he once explained to me, 'never change; only their prices rise and fall.'

All his donkeys are simple, humble, and look exactly alike. Except for one radiant, unique she-donkey he refuses to sell to anyone for any price. She accompanies Sultan al-Karim everywhere. A brave she-donkey with a great secret, who was his guiding light."

"Maybe it's my she-donkey," Fayruz exclaimed upon hearing this.

"Maybe," Musa replied after pondering. "Everyone who sees that she-donkey is sure she was once theirs…" he added. Then he lay back and fell asleep.

28

Heavy clouds covered the sky, and it seemed rain was about to wash everything away. Booming explosions echoed in the distance. Flashes of light shone through the clouds. "It's the storm wind," Fayruz said. "If we don't find her now, she'll vanish forever."

"We must hurry," Musa urged the vast herd, as if anything could change the donkeys' leisurely pace. We trudged slowly up the mountain to meet the great Sultan. Musa led, with Fayruz by his side. Behind them marched the entire donkey herd, and I brought up the rear to ensure no donkey was lost now.

We headed north. The mountains there are so high they kiss the rain clouds. Everyone was excited for the meeting with Sultan al-Kabir. Since the Sultan sold all his donkeys to the Galilee's villagers, the war had closed the border to people and beasts, and no one came here or there anymore. Before reaching the northern high mountains, we had to cross the border.

"We'll need to find a breach in the fence," Musa said, waiting patiently for a way forward. But the donkeys, who dislike borders entirely, grew impatient and rude. They chewed the few rockrose flowers growing among the cracked rocks. It wasn't a proper pasture and couldn't satisfy the herd's ravenous appetite. After finishing the sparse rockroses, they began stomping the rocky ground. They moved nervously, clattering, snorting, pushing each other, and dropping dung…

"They sense the closeness to home," Musa said. "They'll calm down soon."

But then, a tremendous, heart-wrenching bray sounded—the signal the donkeys had been waiting for. At that cue, they charged the border fence and trampled it in one go. They closed their eyes, ignoring the sharp pain of barbed wire and thorns cutting into their flesh.

After crossing the border, the donkeys galloped north. Some carried barbed wire stuck in their flesh, now trailing on the gravel paths, raising clouds of dust. Fayruz paused, studying a map drawn in red ink. "We're here!" she shouted joyfully. "We've reached him."

Before us stood the strange mountain of Sultan al-Kabir.

29

At the mountain's foot, I set down my backpack. Out of habit, I prepared to climb the mountain. I arranged the pitons, hammers, and ropes, but when I looked toward the summit, I couldn't see it.

"I've never seen a mountain like this," I said.

"This mountain has no summit," Musa said, knowing what I sought.

"That means we can climb it, but if it has no summit, we can't conquer it," I explained, setting my climbing gear aside. "I don't need it anymore," I thought. "Nor do I need to conquer the summit. For in Sultan al-Rahim's donkey paradise, other treasures await: Fayruz's she-donkey and the hope that the grey donkeys we've gathered will find a worthy home."

"Here, this mountain seems much lower," Fayruz said, showing us her treasure map.

Musa examined it and said, "That's because the map looks at everything from above."

"What's looking from above?"

"It's when you look down and think you know everything."

"Those who seek treasures must look inward," Fayruz said, closing her turquoise eyes. "The greatest treasures are hidden in the depths."

"How can you look inside a mountain when its rocks are hard and opaque?" Musa asked.

"You can't look inside a mountain," I said, thinking to myself that you can feel its beating heart. For a shepherd's heart knows well what's in a mountain's heart, as all things share one heart.

30

The herd slowly formed a large, noisy grey mass and began marching. After a long hour of walking, Musa stood at the edge of an abyss and declared, "Here it is—the Cave of the Arch."

But we saw no cave or mountain, only a massive stone arch standing over the abyss. We sat on the ground and gazed at the giant arch.

"It's a cave," Musa whispered. "We must be quiet because it's dying now. It's finished its journey and is preparing for the next." Musa sat between us and told us how the great mountain became a stone arch—how it emptied of its rocks and became a cave that grew until it collapsed into itself one day. Soon, what remained would fall, too, and nothing would be left of the great mountain.

"Look how beautiful it is," Musa concluded.

Fayruz looked into Musa's eyes and saw a beauty even greater than that of the stone arch or the sea itself.

"Mountains, too, have a wandering life," Fayruz said, "and even continents and seas, but it's hard to notice because their journeys span hundreds of millions of years. I love watching them on their magnificent journey from here to there. Did you know they sometimes have mixed feelings, too?" she asked Musa.

"I didn't know."

"Of course," she said. "It happens when rockrose flowers crack them open. They know the flowers will crumble them and force them to reveal their secret, but those flowers allow them to set out on their wandering journey."

"Despite their beauty," Musa said, "I don't like these mountains or the stories that come from them. They're opaque and hard, and for some reason, they hide what lies ahead."

"I think they hide the fate of the donkeys and their shepherds," Fayruz said.

"It's not them hiding things from us," Musa said. "Even without the mountains and their strange stories, we, like our donkeys, see almost nothing beyond what's right in front of us—not what has passed or what awaits ahead. Thus, before our eyes and without us noticing, things keep changing... except the grey donkeys," Musa said. "They remain what they are and never change."

"Those changes are dangerous. They do what they want," I said.

"They're inevitable," Fayruz said. "Because at first, they're small and nearly invisible, and by the time you notice them, it's too late to stop them."

"Look at those," Musa said, pointing his staff at some rock rabbits scurrying on the crumbling mountain's stones. "See how afraid they are of change. Nothing is more dangerous to them than these giant rocks when they change," Musa said, his eyes darting to follow the rabbits' frantic movements. "These mountains are unpredictable, and you must be careful when they change, for then they roll stones that crush everything in their path. I once saw a rock collapse and fall on a terrace while two rock rabbits searched for their young. Later, I saw the poor young searching for their parents."

Fayruz's eyes filled with tears at Musa's sad story of the lost young, but she said nothing.

Musa noticed. "What makes mountains change at all?" he asked, trying to shift the topic and cheer her up.

"Persistence," Fayruz said. "Come, look," she invited us. Musa bent down, and I leaned forward to see the persistence. We saw nothing but a small crack in the rock with a tiny flower inside—a delicate, soft purple flower the size of an olive. Musa burst out laughing. "This little persistence can't change anything."

Fayruz flipped through her small notebook and found a page with a dried purple rockrose glued to it.

"Though tiny and shy, the rockrose has tremendous strength," she read aloud. "It drives its roots into cracks and splits the rocks. Thus, it frees them from their grip for their dangerous journey down the mountain slopes."

"You're reading upside down again," Musa said, but this time he didn't turn the notebook. He understood now. A smile shone through Fayruz's eyes.

"I didn't know rocks go on journeys," I said.

"It's a long and unique journey, where rocks slide from mountain tops to valleys and then to streams. Water and winds erode and crumble them until they turn to dust. And when donkeys tread the mountain paths, the dust rises with the wind and flies lightly to other lands... Without that small flower, they'd cling to their place and never change. Only the donkeys see clearly what lies before them and bother to understand the little they see. So, despite their hunger, they don't eat these soft, beautiful rockrose flowers."

"Maybe that's what the big rocks try so hard to hide—that they fear change," Musa said.

"I didn't know mountains change and disappear, or that caves can die," I said to my shepherd friends.

Even the pastures were once mountains before they wandered and became the plains they are now. I still remember they were once mountains and honor them for it, calling them mountains. And the mountains were once green pastures, for the life of wanderers never stops. It only changes.

31

"Let's bid farewell to the mountain," Musa said as it grew late.

"Is it sad to part?" Fayruz asked.

"I don't resist parting, so it's neither sad nor painful for me," Musa replied.

And I thought of people and distant places. Of my beloved home, whose fate I didn't know—whether it still stood. Of my loved ones and the inevitable separation the war had forced upon us. How I wished they were here by my side.

We stood in a moment of silence for the magnificent mountain that once passed through here, leaving us only an arch of stones as a parting gift.

"Where do you end up if you cross to the other side?" I asked.

"Nowhere," Musa said. "Herds always march to nowhere."

"Every place is nowhere if it lacks a shepherd's tune," Fayruz read from her ancient notebook.

I recalled all the places I'd been. All the grueling climbs to mountain peaks. How I labored in vain on my long journey to the highest summits—to Kala Patthar, Aconcagua, Kilimanjaro, and all the other lofty peaks I reached through arduous climbs. And how they were all nowhere, just like any other nowhere, only to find in them what I brought myself. Now, I couldn't quite understand why I chose to climb mountains with pitons, ropes, and calculated risks. Perhaps, I thought, what makes these places special is the effort we're willing to invest to reach them.

32

From the wadi below, somewhere in the abyss, rose the sounds of flocks and people.

A vast caravan of thousands of war survivors made their journey there. They looked sad and weary, carrying the little they had left on their backs. A tribe of unfortunate battered people gathered from across the Galilee. Some limped, struggling to move from place to place. Among them were the blind and those whose hope had been lost. Some bore burns. There were the elderly and the sick, women carrying tender infants in their arms, and one child without a leg.

"They're fleeing the storm wind," Fayruz whispered. To her, they seemed like a plea for help—people struck by the storm wind who had given up on their inner donkey. For a moment, all the hardships of the journey, the worry for her radiant she-donkey, and the longing faded. Her own troubles vanished in the face of their sorrow and pain. "A shepherd is one with worry in their heart," she recalled. Now, the worry nesting in her heart urged her to act. If only she knew how to help them. And all these wondrous donkeys here with her—if only she could give them to these people. Though so simple and flawed, how much light they could bring… But an abyss separated us from them, and Fayruz didn't know how to cross it.

"The storm wind is closing in," Musa called, snapping Fayruz from her daydream. "It's dangerous, and we need to get out of here fast."
"This abyss is just as dangerous. How do we cross the narrow bridge of the Cave of the Arch without falling?" Fayruz asked.
"We'll take a calculated risk," I suggested.
"That calculation is very risky," Fayruz warned, pulling out the old map drawn in red ink, neatly folded between the pages of her notebook. "If you stick to calculations, you end up taking no risks and never arrive. And we're so close to Afifa's treasure," she said, stepping onto the narrow bridge of the Cave of the Arch.

Musa looked at the map. A dotted line marked the path from Afifa's home to some mysterious treasure marked there. According to the map, it lay among the roots of an ancient tree on the peak of a mighty mountain. "Exactly according to plan," Musa said.

Fayruz gathered three rockrose seeds, caressed them, and tucked them into a fold of her galabiya. "Sometimes you need to split a mountain to reach the treasure," she whispered to us, sending each of us a playful wink.

33

We ran… The storm wind approached swiftly, carrying the smell of smoke and the roaring sound of explosions. We chased the galloping herd up the mountain, worry in our hearts. We passed through the heavy clouds hiding the mountain's peak and climbed higher until the place where all that was lost was revealed. Here, at the mountain's top, stood a tree unlike any we'd ever seen. Yellow, sticky tears dripped down its trunk. Beside the tree stood the white tent of Sultan al-Karim Rahman.

"It's a mastic tree," Musa said, "the last one left."
Sultan al-Karim emerged from the tent, revealed before us—a dignified elder in a white robe, his face adorned with a cloud of soft, white beard. He looked at us as if he already knew everything.
"For those who love Rahat Lokum, there's no greater treasure than the mastic of this old tree," he said in his booming voice. "But it seems only Afifa and the donkeys know that."
"I knew I'd find a treasure here," Fayruz said. She folded her treasure map drawn in red ink and tucked it between the pages of

her notebook. And I remembered Afifa and the treasures she had everywhere.

"Here they are," the Sultan declared joyfully as he noticed our herd, "all my treasures," he said, as if he were the master of all the donkeys.

We stood and watched him. He surveyed the herd patiently, moving from donkey to donkey, caressing each one and whispering something in their ears. When he finished, he looked at us—a weary, strange bunch: two shepherds and a mountaineer.

From afar, the storm wind roared, wreaking havoc and fear on everything in its path. On the strange mountain with no peak, silence fell. Donkeys, plants, and people stood still.

A donkey's bray came from the white tent. Fayruz thought she recognized the sound.

"Maybe you've seen my she-donkey," Fayruz dared to ask the Sultan.

The Sultan looked into her turquoise eyes and didn't answer.

"It's been a long time since I've seen her..." Fayruz said, her voice choked.

"No," the Sultan replied curtly, as if hiding something.

"I heard," Fayruz said hesitantly, "about a radiant she-donkey that accompanies you..."

"Yes, ya binti (my daughter), that's the she-donkey within me," al-Karim said in his compassionate, merciful way.

He closed his eyes and took a deep breath. "If you want to see her, do as I do," he suggested. Fayruz closed her eyes and breathed inward. In the inner darkness, she suddenly saw a radiant she-donkey. Glowing and unique, yet so like all the other donkeys. One moment grey and ordinary, the next radiant and majestic. Her eyes were large, clear, and full of donkey wisdom, adorned with beautiful white patches. She wore two joyful, long ears, turning them this way and that, as if looking through them at a world that was a strange riddle. Her right ear turned forward, her left backward, as if she couldn't decide what mattered more—what had passed or what lay ahead. Her eyes sank deep into what lay before her now, fixed on a huge pile of yellow hay.

"Isn't she wonderful?" the Sultan said, smiling.
"Yes!" Fayruz agreed. "She was with me all along. Our donkeys are always with us. I thought I wasn't worthy, so I couldn't see her."

34

Musa said his task was complete. A single grey she-donkey stepped forward slowly, parting the herd, and stood by his side.

"Farewell, beloved shepherds," he said, turning to leave.

"Just one more moment," Fayruz pleaded.

She approached the grey she-donkey and hugged her neck, caressed her forehead, and kissed her gently. The she-donkey rubbed her head against Fayruz's arm, sniffing the last cube of Rahat Lokum in her pocket. Fayruz pulled it out and cut it in half. She placed one half in the she-donkey's mouth and gave the other to Musa.

"I want to look at you one last time," Fayruz requested.

Musa approached her and gently removed the long scarf covering her face. He looked one last time into her turquoise eyes, seeing in them what he was. Fayruz smiled at him, then gave him a sweet kiss—sweeter than Rahat Lokum or anything he'd ever tasted.

"You saved me," she said, "from neglect and blindness."

"It's nothing," Musa said, wiping her eyes.

"My she-donkey wants me to continue the wandering journey," Musa said.

The grey she-donkey shook her gull-wing ears back and forth, flapping them in agreement.

"Our feelings will be mixed forever," Musa promised.

He placed a red headscarf on the she-donkey's head, tied a short rope to her, and smiled a farewell smile at Fayruz. He bowed deeply to the Sultan in respect and gratitude, then whispered a shepherd's whisper into the she-donkey's ear. Together, they descended into the valley and vanished.

A bray of longing echoed through the great valley. The vast herd bid farewell, in its own way, to Musa and his donkey as they faded into the distance. The donkeys stood side by side as a great mass, silently chewing the sweet grass growing on the slopes of Sultan al-Karim's high mountain. A gentle evening breeze rose from the sea, carrying a delicate, enchanting tune of a small shepherd's flute. A simple melody that reminded Fayruz that things, on their own, are nothing, but we can fill them with a shepherd's song. We make things what they are.

35

When the donkeys' farewell song subsided, Sultan al-Rahman moved among all his grey donkeys. He caressed their heads and tended to the wounds cut into their flesh by barbed wire fences.

"What shall we do with so many donkeys? They could bring so much happiness to so many shepherds, if only they knew how to love them," he said.

"I fear there's no one left in the Galilee to love them..." Fayruz said, but then remembered the caravan of storm wind survivors. "If you permit, I'll take them to another place. There, they'll bring happiness to other shepherds who yearn for it. I'll be a worthy shepherd to them," she promised.

"And your she-donkey? What about her?"

"She'll always be within me, my radiant she-donkey, carrying my dreams, my loves, my longings, and my mixed feelings... And I'll always remember she's the one who makes me who I am—a shepherd with worry in her heart... for the donkeys and their shepherds."

"So be it!" the Sultan said. "Come, let's prepare you for the wandering journey."

Then, Fayruz packed all the Rahat Lokum al-Karim gave her and bid him farewell. She clucked a few times, and the donkeys raised their heads and looked at her. She closed her eyes, pursed her lips, and gently blew a shepherd's whistle, unlike any ever heard on the snowy peaks of Lebanon.

We marched down the mountain together. I, on my way to continue my wandering journey, and Fayruz with the wondrous herd, heading toward the caravan of survivors. The descent reminded me of all the peaks I'd conquered while fleeing the war outside and the storm wind within me, searching for treasures and finding, in the end, a humble grey donkey. This brought a smile to my face.

Fayruz removed the scarf from her face and smiled back at me, embarrassed. Something seemed to trouble her soul.

"Though he's a rascal, this donkey of mine," I said to ease the awkwardness, "I love him and trust him deeply."

"He's a charming grey donkey," Fayruz replied. "And it seems I neglected the she-donkey within me, letting her become wild and hurt those who loved me most."

"You mean yourself?!"

"I mean Afifa…" Fayruz said, pulling the small notebook from her galabiya. "Only when I saw the caravan of survivors did I realize I took from her what wasn't mine… I caused her worry and harm. I thought I'd find answers to my questions in it… When I closed my eyes and saw my radiant she-donkey, I knew I should have sought them within myself and on the journey with you. I'm so ashamed," she said, covering her face with the scarf again.

"If you wish, I'll return it to her," I offered.

"Will you ask her forgiveness on my behalf?"

"I promise," I said.

We walked down together, a gentle breeze caressing our sweaty faces. I gazed at the horizon, pondering the beauty of winding paths. Fayruz dreamed awake, seemingly looking inward. Slowly, light returned to her turquoise eyes. As if sharing a precious treasure, she described to me the beauty and virtues of the she-donkey within her. Then, she touched the small wrinkle between my brows with her fingertip and smiled, and I knew for certain I'd become a worthy shepherd.

When we finished descending the mountain, we each went our separate ways. I watched her as she faded from me forever—a kindhearted, incomparably beautiful shepherd with turquoise eyes, dressed in a grey galabiya and a simple scarf, carrying her radiant she-donkey in her heart, followed by a vast herd of grey donkeys ready to bring happiness, leaving behind a cloud of trail dust.

Since then, no grey donkeys have been seen in the Galilee. No one knows where those wondrous creatures went—strange, unassuming beings. Perhaps they returned somewhere to that mountain with no peak, to be with all that was lost. Perhaps they found worthy shepherds and bring them great happiness.

If you're fortunate enough to have such a grey donkey, be generous to it and don't hide it. Embrace it in your heart and love it as it is. There's no need to lose it to realize how precious it is to you. And for those with a wild one… Allah yirhamu (may God have mercy).

EPILOGUE

It seems there's no recipe book powerful enough to answer all questions. But don't be saddened. As shepherds, you have the power to fill everything with your own song. Open your eyes and see! Here, among you, is a wise grey donkey, waiting for you to notice it, meanwhile chewing in boredom the straw and chaff you've given it.

Be good shepherds to it. Care for it with love and devotion, and when the time comes for it to continue its journey, follow it! It's very possible that somewhere, at the journey's end, you'll find a treasure or a small cube of Rahat Lokum.

May we see our grey donkeys clearly and become worthy shepherds to them.

Before we parted, Fayruz wrote down the Shepherd's Guide for me and asked me to share it, at my discretion, with anyone who needs it.

What's the point? I thought. The shepherds of the Galilee have no time to read. But I did as she instructed. I tore a page from Afifa's notebook, wrote "Shepherd's Guide" at the top, and transcribed what Fayruz dictated.

If you need it, here it is in her words:

The Shepherd's Guide

Recognize it!
Everyone has a donkey to guide them on the way. Though shortsighted, donkeys see what lies directly ahead better than we do.

Know it!
Your donkey, though grey like its fellows, is unique and unlike any other.

Nurture it!
You cannot love a donkey without nurturing it. (Nor can you nurture a donkey without loving it.)

Trust it!
A donkey never moves from place to place in a straight line, for the right path is long and winding. Those who wish to walk straight need no donkey. Hold the rope and follow it to get lost safely.

Set it free!
Those who give their donkey freedom and trust it are guaranteed to reach wondrous places. Never argue with your donkey; there's no need to reach an agreement.

Give it all it wants!
Donkeys know well the difference between what they need and what they want, and they follow only what they truly need, sadly giving up their wants easily. Give them what they want—for that's what you truly need.

Let it be what it is!
Don't try to change it. In a world that's always changing, the donkey never changes.

Act for it!
Pave the way to its heart with actions, not words.

Forgive it!

Donkeys don't take offense. If you've hurt your donkey, there's no need to apologize. Forgive yourself, and it will forgive you.

Be good!

Donkeys don't ask us to be the best, but they expect us to do our very best.

Don't worry for it!

Donkeys have no real enemies except neglect and foolishness, and even those they never fear.

Don't rush it!

It has its own pace, and you can't hurry it. If you have patience, it will take you safely to wondrous places.

Don't ride it!

Happiness is already where you are. To be happy, you don't need to ride anywhere, and they're not meant for riding anyway.

On the other side of the torn page, I found a recipe for a wonderful treat. Nothing is more beloved to donkeys than this sweet. Here's the recipe for making Rahat Lokum. (The recipe has been adapted for kitchens where mastic tree resin is unavailable.)

Ingredients:

- 3½ cups water for the syrup + 1 cup water for mixing the cornstarch
- 4 cups white sugar
- Pinch of salt
- ⅔ tsp citric acid
- ½ cup cornstarch
- 2 tbsp rose water
- ⅓ cup powdered sugar mixed with 1 flat tbsp cornstarch, for dusting the Rahat Lokum cubes

Instructions:

1. Line a 20x30 cm rectangular silicone mold with a double layer of aluminum foil, with edges protruding to ease removal of the treat, and grease with butter or oil.
2. Prepare the syrup: Place sugar, salt, and citric acid in a double-bottomed pot. Stir while cooking until all ingredients melt and form a light syrup. Remove from heat.
3. Mix the water and cornstarch thoroughly until smooth, with no lumps. Pour into the syrup and whisk well.
4. Return the pot to the heat and bring to a boil, stirring constantly until the mixture thickens and bubbles. Lower the heat and cook, stirring continuously, for 45

minutes. Scrape the pot's bottom to prevent the starch from sticking or the treat from burning. The mixture will thicken significantly and change from cloudy to clear with a light amber hue.

5. Add the rose water, stir for another minute, and remove from heat. Pour the mixture into the mold and smooth with a spatula or spoon. Tap the mold several times on a marble surface to release air bubbles.
6. Let cool completely and set for at least 2-3 hours.
7. Remove the treat from the mold. Cut the flexible treat into 2x2 cm cubes. Roll the cubes in the powdered sugar and cornstarch mixture and store in a single layer in an airtight container dusted generously with the same mixture. The treat will keep well for two weeks.

Store in a cool, shaded place, as far as possible from grey donkeys.

THE END

Made in United States
North Haven, CT
05 September 2025

72432932R00059